77

BIBLE VERSES

TO GROW ON

(With 77 Poems)

CAROLYN WILDE

77 Bible Verses

to Grow On

With 77 Poems

ISBN - 9780615794914

Printed in the United States of America

2013 by Carolyn Wilde

Additional Books May Be Obtained
by Contacting:

Carolyn Wilde

PO Box 1321, Foley, AL 36536

Email: pcwilde@gulftel.com

Web site: newlifeinchristchurch.net

TABLE OF CONTENTS

1. Jeremiah 17:9
2. Romans 6:23
3. Proverbs 3:5-6
4. Isaiah 12:3
5. John 6:37
6. Proverbs 18:10
7. Matthew 6:33
8. II Corinthians 1:20
9. Exodus 23:2
10. Galatians 6:9
11. Matthew 5:9
12. Philippians 4:6
13. Philippians 4:13
14. Ephesians 4:26
15. John 16:33
16. Psalms 119:11
17. Psalms 101:3
18. Ecclesiastes 12:1
19. Hebrews 13:5
20. I Corinthians 10:13
21. James 3:8
22. Proverbs 19:17
23. I Peter 2:2
24. John 13:14
25. Romans 13:8
26. Ephesians 6:1
27. Galatians 6:2
28. Galatians 6:1
29. Matthew 6:15
30. I Corinthians 6:19
31. I Corinthians 11:24
32. Matthew 26:30
33. Colossians 3:17
34. John 14:26
35. Colossians 1:27
36. Malachi 3:16-17
37. Exodus 3:14
38. Ecclesiastes 5:5
39. Isaiah 57:20
40. Habakkuk 2:3
41. Romans 12:2
42. Psalms 133:1
43. Zechariah 13:1
44. Psalms 46:2
45. Zephaniah 3:17
46. John 2:5
47. I John 2:15
48. Philippians 4:8
49. Jude 1:24
50. Isaiah 12:2
51. Proverbs 23:4-5
52. II Corinthians 7:1
53. James 4:14
54. James 2:19
55. Psalms 14:1
56. Proverbs 16:16
57. Isaiah 40:11
58. Luke 13:3
59. Matthew 3:11-12
60. I Timothy 6:20-21
61. I Peter 5:7
62. Ephesians 4:32
63. Proverbs 4:14-15
64. Mark 8:38
65. Revelation 3:20
66. Romans 13:12
67. Psalms 23:3
68. Romans 2:8
69. II Corinthians 6:14
70. I Thessalonians 5:22
71. Luke 6:46
72. II Corinthians 5:7
73. John 5:24
74. Jeremiah 12:5
75. II Corinthians 12:9
76. Isaiah 60:2
77. Matthew 6:20

All Scriptures are taken from the King James Bible.

"Thy word is a lamp unto my feet, and a light unto my path."
Psalm 119:105

"The entrance of thy words giveth light; it giveth understanding unto the simple." Psalm 119:130

"How sweet are thy words unto my taste! yea, sweeter than honey to my mouth!" Psalm 119:103

"For ever, O Lord, thy word is settled in heaven." Psalm 119:89

"Thy word is very pure: therefore thy servant loveth it." Psalm 119:140

A Note from Carolyn ...

This is not a book to read quickly from cover to cover.

It is a book to read just one page at a time.

These 77 verses should not be read and forgotten.

These 77 verses should be stored in our hearts and remembered.

As we make our journey through life, we need God's Word to guide us. Many have given their lives down through the centuries to deliver it to us.

It is the true wealth in this world.

May this small book be a blessing to you.

One

"The heart is deceitful above all things, and desperately wicked: who can know it?"
Jeremiah 17:9

I will follow You,

my Lord,

And I'll make a brand

new start;

I will no longer follow

my deceitful, wicked heart.

Two

"For the wages of sin is death; but the gift of God is eternal life through Jesus Christ our Lord." *Romans 6:23*

The life of sin

surely does pay;

It earns man death

on judgment day.

Three

"Trust in the Lord with all thine heart; and lean not unto thine own understanding. In all thy ways acknowledge him, and he shall direct thy paths."
Proverbs 3:5-6

When I trust in my Lord

Who knows each tomorrow;

He will direct my path

And save me much sorrow.

Four

"Therefore with joy shall ye draw water out of the wells of salvation."
Isaiah 12:3

With joy I answer

my dear Savior's call!

I run to His well!

Salvation I draw!

Five

"All that the Father giveth me shall come to me; and him that cometh to me I will in no wise cast out."
John 6:37

I came believing

He didn't cast me out!

This wonderful promise

just cast out all doubt!

Six

"The name of the Lord is a strong tower: the righteous runneth into it, and is safe." *Proverbs 18:10*

His beautiful name

has all His power.

Sweet place of safety;

It's my High Tower.

Seven

"But seek ye first the kingdom of God, and his righteousness; and all these things shall be added unto you." *Matthew 6:33*

When I do my part

and seek my Lord first;

For all of my needs

I never will thirst.

Eight

"For all the promises of God in him are yea, and in him Amen, unto the glory of God by us." *II Corinthians 1:20*

To all God's promises,

I say "Yea" and "Amen"!

Now I just trust in Him

to know the "Where"

and "When"!

Nine

"Thou shalt not follow a multitude to do evil."

Exodus 23:2

This warning to us

does surely advise,

To follow the crowd

Will never be wise.

Ten

"And let us not be weary in well doing: for in due season we shall reap, if we faint not." *Galatians 6:9*

Keep doing well

without complaint,

Reaping will come,

if you don't faint.

Eleven

"Blessed are the peacemakers: for they shall be called the children of God." *Matthew 5:9*

The Father's children

In love make sweet peace.

For each bitter grudge

they quickly release.

Twelve

"Be careful for nothing; but in every thing by prayer and supplication with thanksgiving let your requests be made known unto God." *Philippians 4:6*

Do not be burdened;

Loaded down with care;

Take every worry

To the Lord in prayer.

Thirteen

"I can do all things through Christ which strengtheneth me." *Philippians 4:13*

God's Word, prayer,

and fasting

Give me strength

for this hour.

I can do each of them

When I call on

Christ's power.

Fourteen

"Be ye angry, and sin not: let not the sun go down upon your wrath." *Ephesians 4:26*

'Ere the sun ends

its daily path,

Let love prevail -

let go your wrath.

Fifteen

"These things I have spoken unto you, that in me ye might have peace. In the world ye shall have tribulation: but be of good cheer; I have overcome the world." *John 16:33*

When trouble comes,

Be of good cheer!

"Have peace, My Child,

I am still here."

Sixteen

"Thy word have I hid in mine heart, that I might not sin against thee."
Psalms 119:11

When I deposit God's

Word in my heart,

Sinning against God

will swiftly depart.

Seventeen

"I will set no wicked thing before mine eyes: I hate the work of them that turn aside; it shall not cleave to me." *Psalms 101:3*

I won't pollute the eyes

God made for me to see!

So not one wicked thing

will I set before me!

Eighteen

"Remember now thy Creator in the days of thy youth, while the evil days come not, nor the years draw nigh, when thou shalt say, I have no pleasure in them."

Ecclesiastes 12:1

Do not wait until youth is fully spent;
To answer God's call
And go where He's sent.

Nineteen

"Let your conversation be without covetousness; and be content with such things as ye have: for he hath said, I will never leave thee, nor forsake thee." *Hebrews 13:5*

What things can this world

offer to my heart;

Compared to my Lord

Who will never depart?

Twenty

"There hath no temptation taken you but such as is common to man: but God is faithful, who will not suffer you to be tempted above that ye are able; but will with the temptation also make a way to escape, that ye may be able to bear it."
I Corinthians 10:13

If escape from sin

You are looking for;

Just run to Jesus!

For He is the Door!

Twenty-One

"But the tongue can no man tame; it is an unruly evil, full of deadly poison."
James 3:8

So many by my words

have been poisoned

and stung,

I should have asked You,

Lord,

to tame my deadly tongue.

Twenty-Two

"He that hath pity upon the poor lendeth unto the Lord; and that which he hath given will he pay him again."

Proverbs 19:17

When I give to the one

who cannot food afford;

The gift is but a loan,

That's paid back

by the Lord.

Twenty-Three

"As newborn babes, desire the sincere milk of the word, that ye may grow thereby."

I Peter 2:2

As a babe desires milk

so he can live and grow;

When I want to be fed,

to the Lord's Word I go.

Twenty-Four

"If I then, your Lord and Master, have washed your feet; ye also ought to wash one another's feet."
John 13:14

Jesus knelt to wash feet,

The King of kings is He!

Lord, I will follow You!

I'll serve. I'm here!

Use me!

Twenty-Five

"Owe no man any thing, but to love one another: for he that loveth another hath fulfilled the law."

Romans 13:8

To every one,

our debt's the same;

To love his soul,

in Jesus' name.

Twenty-Six

"Children, obey your parents in the Lord: for this is right."

Ephesians 6:1

"Children, obey your

parents."

This is so easy to say.

Then I stop and ask

myself:

Do I my Father obey?

Twenty-Seven

"Bear ye one another's burdens, and so fulfil the law of Christ." *Galatians 6:2*

Go to your burdened brother;

But don't criticize and scold.

You must, to fulfil Christ's law,

Just help him; his burden hold.

Twenty-Eight

"Brethren, if a man be overtaken in a fault, ye which are spiritual, restore such an one in the spirit of meekness; considering thyself, lest thou also be tempted." *Galatians 6:1*

When you're restoring others,

remember to be humble;

Or you may find that your fault

Will soon cause you to stumble.

Twenty-Nine

"But if ye forgive not men their trespasses, neither will your Father forgive your trespasses." *Matthew 6:15*

You refused to listen to My Word that is true. You refused to forgive, So I won't forgive you!

Thirty

"What? know ye not that your body is the temple of the Holy Ghost which is in you, which ye have of God, and ye are not your own?"
I Corinthians 6:19

To waste all my days

serving self is wrong;

For my Lord bought me,

To Him I belong.

Thirty-One

"And when he had given thanks, he brake it, and said, Take, eat: this is my body, which is broken for you: this do in remembrance of me."

I Corinthians 11:24

He gave thanks for His
body, that cruel men
would soon break.
Then died for
our salvation;
Now invites us to partake.

Thirty-Two

"And when they had sung an hymn, they went out into the mount of Olives."

Matthew 26:30

Before He went to

the Garden,

Where He poured sweat as

blood, and cried;

Our Lord took time to

sing a hymn,

Then He went to the cross,

and died.

Thirty-Three

"And whatsoever ye do in word or deed, do all in the name of the Lord Jesus, giving thanks to God and the Father by him."
Colossians 3:17

Jesus, I so want to live,

in Your precious name

today;

May all my deeds please

You, Lord;

And bless every word

I say.

Thirty-Four

"But the Comforter, which is the Holy Ghost, whom the Father will send in my name, he shall teach you all things, and bring all things to your remembrance, whatsoever I have said unto you."
John 14:26

God's Breath blowing on me

is Heaven's pure

white Dove,

Here to bring me comfort,

From my Father of love.

Thirty-Five

"To whom God would make known what is the riches of the glory of this mystery among the Gentiles; which is Christ in you, the hope of glory." *Colossians 1:27*

My one hope of glory
Is Christ, alive in me!
Oh! How rich is His Gift;
This wondrous mystery!

Thirty-Six

"Then they that feared the Lord spake often one to another: and the Lord hearkened, and heard it, and a book of remembrance was written before him for them that feared the Lord, and that thought upon his name. And they shall be mine, saith the Lord of hosts, in that day when I make up my jewels; and I will spare them, as a man spareth his own son that serveth him."
Malachi 3:16-17

Yes, I do fear my Lord.

I love His precious name.

By doing only these,

His jewel I became!

Thirty-Seven

"And God said unto Moses, I AM THAT I AM: and he said, Thus shalt thou say unto the children of Israel, I AM hath sent me unto you."

Exodus 3:14

He is Life; Water; Light; and God's beloved Lamb. The Answer to man's need is in the great "I AM"!

Thirty-Eight

"Better is it that thou shouldest not vow, than that thou shouldest vow and not pay." *Ecclesiastes 5:5*

It is far better

A vow not to speak.

Than make a promise

That you do not keep.

Thirty-Nine

"But the wicked are like the troubled sea, when it cannot rest, whose waters cast up mire and dirt." *Isaiah 57:20*

As the raging waters

of tossed and troubled sea;

No rest for the wicked

who will not bend the knee.

Forty

"For the vision is yet for an appointed time, but at the end it shall speak, and not lie: though it tarry, wait for it; because it will surely come, it will not tarry."

Habakkuk 2:3

Each promise in Your book,

Lord, will one day

come true.

So help me have patience,

And keep on trusting You.

Forty-One

"And be not conformed to this world: but be ye transformed by the renewing of your mind, that ye may prove what is that good, and acceptable, and perfect, will of God." **Romans 12:2**

To this wicked world

I will not conform.

I give You my mind,

For You to transform.

Forty-Two

"Behold, how good and how pleasant it is for brethren to dwell together in unity!"
Psalm 133:1

Dear Lord, as You

look down, from Your

throne up above,

May You find me dwelling

with Your family, in love.

Forty-Three

"In that day there shall be a fountain opened to the house of David and to the inhabitants of Jerusalem for sin and for uncleanness."
Zechariah 13:1

A fountain of blood

poured from God's

dear Son;

Washed my sins away;

My freedom He won!

Forty-Four

"Therefore will not we fear, though the earth be removed, and though the mountains be carried into the midst of the sea."
Psalms 46:2

Tho' the earth be removed,

we should yet have no fear;

Our Lord is holding us,

And He will still be here!

Forty-Five

"The Lord thy God in the midst of thee is mighty; he will save, he will rejoice over thee with joy; he will rest in his love, he will joy over thee with singing."
Zephaniah 3:17

My loving, gentle Father,

singing Your baby to sleep;

I rest safely in Your arms;

I know my soul

You will keep.

Forty-Six

"His mother saith unto the servants, whatsoever he saith unto you, do it." *John 2:5*

This advice from Mary,

is still for us today.

So you who serve the Lord,

Just simply Him obey!

Forty-Seven

"Love not the world, neither the things that are in the world. If any man love the world, the love of the Father is not in him." *I John 2:15*

To choose heav'n

above hell

is such an easy task.

But heav'n above

this world

is what our Lord

does ask.

Forty-Eight

"Finally, brethren, whatsoever things are true, whatsoever things are honest, whatsoever things are just, whatsoever things are pure, whatsoever things are lovely, whatsoever things are of good report; if there be any virtue, and if there be any praise, think on these things." *Philippians 4:8*

Things true, pure,

and lovely,

we're told to think about.

Today's entertainment,

we'd better just throw out!

Forty-Nine

"Now unto him that is able to keep you from falling, and to present you faultless before the presence of his glory with exceeding joy."

Jude 1:24

The wonder of salvation!

Upheld by our Lord's

strong hand!

A sinner declared faultless,

when before His throne

I stand!

Fifty

"Behold, God is my salvation; I will trust, and not be afraid: for the Lord Jehovah is my strength and my song; he also is become my salvation."
Isaiah 12:2

I can trust no one, Lord - myself, man, or nation.

You alone are my strength, my song, my salvation!

Fifty-One

"Labour not to be rich: cease from thine own wisdom. Wilt thou set thine eyes upon that which is not? for riches certainly make themselves wings; they fly away as an eagle toward heaven."
Proverbs 23:4-5

As a bird flies away,

So earth's riches go too.

Ev'ry soul who has died

now knows that this is true.

Fifty-Two

"Having therefore these promises, dearly beloved, let us cleanse ourselves from all filthiness of the flesh and spirit, perfecting holiness in the fear of God."

II Corinthians 7:1

Father, I don't want

You to disapprove;

From flesh and spirit,

filth I now remove.

Fifty-Three

"Whereas ye know not what shall be on the morrow. For what is your life? It is even a vapour, that appeareth for a little time, and then vanisheth away." *James 4:14*

My life is but a vapor,

so I need to work

this day;

To do God's will;

seek Him first;

Love all my neighbors;

and pray!

Fifty-Four

"Thou believest that there is one God; thou doest well: the devils also believe, and tremble." *James 2:19*

It is not enough

To only believe;

Jesus, my Savior,

I must now receive.

Fifty-Five

"The fool hath said in his heart, There is no God. They are corrupt, they have done abominable works, there is none that doeth good."

Psalms 14:1

How dare we remove God
and His Word
from our schools?
We'll only educate
a crop of corrupt fools!

Fifty-Six

"How much better is it to get wisdom than gold! and to get understanding rather to be chosen than silver!"

Proverbs 16:16

Better is wisdom

Than all of earth's gold,

For which many men

Their own souls have sold.

Fifty-Seven

"He shall feed his flock like a shepherd: he shall gather the lambs with his arm, and carry them in his bosom, and shall gently lead those that are with young." *Isaiah 40:11*

I trust my Shepherd's arm
To care for me and feed;
To gently carry me
And to heav'n safely lead.

Fifty-Eight

"I tell you, Nay: but, except ye repent, ye shall all likewise perish."
Luke 13:3

How shall I escape

this sure death sentence?

There's only one way;

It's true repentance.

Fifty-Nine

"... he shall baptize you with the Holy Ghost, and with fire: whose fan is in his hand, and he will throughly purge his floor, and gather his wheat into the garner; but he will burn up the chaff with unquenchable fire."
Matthew 3:11-12

Father, I call on You,

in Jesus' blessed name!

Burn up all chaff in me,

Send Your Spirit's

holy flame!

Sixty

"O Timothy, keep that which is committed to thy trust, avoiding profane and vain babblings, and oppositions of science falsely so called: which some professing have erred concerning the faith."
I Timothy 6:20-21

My God, my Creator,

It's on You I now call;

May lies of false science

never cause me to fall.

Sixty-One

"Casting all your care upon him; for he careth for you."

I Peter 5:7

All of my problems

are too hard to bear;

So I cast on God

Each and ev'ry care.

Sixty-Two

"And be ye kind one to another, tenderhearted, forgiving one another, even as God for Christ's sake hath forgiven you."
Ephesians 4:32

A beautiful rule

for Christ-like living;

Have tender, kind hearts,

Always forgiving.

Sixty-Three

"Enter not into the path of the wicked, and go not in the way of evil men. Avoid it, pass not by it, turn from it, and pass away."

Proverbs 4:14-15

This proverb is a truth
Ev'ry Christian must know.
Never with evil men
Should you consent to go.

Sixty-Four

"**Whosoever therefore shall be ashamed of me and of my words in this adulterous and sinful generation; of him also shall the Son of man be ashamed, when he cometh in the glory of his Father with the holy angels.**" *Mark 8:38*

If ashamed of your Savior,

Who died

on the rugged cross,

When He comes

In His glory,

You'll suffer eternal loss.

Sixty-Five

"Behold, I stand at the door, and knock: if any man hear my voice, and open the door, I will come in to him, and will sup with him, and he with me. Inasmuch as ye did it not to one of the least of these, ye did it not to me." *Rev. 3:20 + Matt. 25:45*

Members of the lukewarm church, meeting in His precious name:

Hear! He's knocking at the door, as the sick, the poor, and lame.

Sixty-Six

"The night is far spent, the day is at hand: let us therefore cast off the works of darkness, and let us put on the armour of light."

Romans 13:12

The day is coming!

Nearly gone the night!

Drive back sin's darkness,

with Armour of Light!

Sixty-Seven

"He restoreth my soul: he leadeth me in the paths of righteousness for his name's sake." *Psalm 23:3*

Lord, You have a righteous,

and good and holy name.

I pray that I, Your child,

Will never bring You shame.

Sixty-Eight

"But unto them that are contentious, and do not obey the truth, but obey unrighteousness, indignation and wrath." *Romans 2:8*

Father, I choose now

to walk,

down the obedient path;

I forsake unrighteousness;

So I now escape

Your wrath.

Sixty-Nine

"Be ye not unequally yoked together with unbelievers: for what fellowship hath righteousness with unrighteousness? and what communion hath light with darkness?" *II Corinthians 6:14*

If you are yoked to one

who is not your brother;

You'll be pulling one way,

and he'll pull another.

Seventy

"Abstain from all appearance of evil."
I Thessalonians 5:22

If it looks like evil,

run away at all cost;

Or you may discover

your reputation lost.

Seventy-One

"And why call ye me, Lord, Lord, and do not the things which I say?" *Luke 6:46*

It's not enough just mere words to say;

When Jesus is Lord,

I must obey!

Seventy-Two

"For we walk by faith, not by sight." *II Corinthians 5:7*

Just one path to walk

is good and is right;

It's the path of faith,

not the one of sight.

Seventy-Three

"Verily, verily, I say unto you, He that heareth my word, and believeth on him that sent me, hath everlasting life, and shall not come into condemnation; but is passed from death unto life." *John 5:24*

When I look into
my Savior's dear face,
No condemnation!
Just amazing grace!

Seventy-Four

"If thou hast run with the footmen, and they have wearied thee, then how canst thou contend with horses? and if in the land of peace, wherein thou trustedst, they wearied thee, then how wilt thou do in the swelling of Jordan?" *Jeremiah 12:5*

You're tired already,

as you run life's race?

What will you do at

the increasing pace?

Seventy-Five

"And he said unto me, My grace is sufficient for thee: for my strength is made perfect in weakness. Most gladly therefore will I rather glory in my infirmities, that the power of Christ may rest upon me." *II Corinthians 12:9*

Lord, I am weary!
My race has been long.
But when I am weak,
I find You are strong!

Seventy-Six

"For, behold, the darkness shall cover the earth, and gross darkness the people: but the Lord shall arise upon thee, and his glory shall be seen upon thee."
Isaiah 60:2

When earth grows

more wicked

And in gross darkness lies,

God's glory will be seen;

On His saints He will rise!

Seventy-Seven

"But lay up for yourselves treasures in heaven, where neither moth nor rust doth corrupt, and where thieves do not break through nor steal." *Matthew 6:20*

What treasures can I send

to my home up above?

Only souls,

bought with blood, and

our dear Savior's love.

John 12:48

"He that rejecteth me, and receiveth not my words, hath one that judgeth him: the word that I have spoken, the same shall judge him in the last day."

Jesus

A Final Word

And so, My Dear Friend,
What now will you do?
Obey the Lord's Word,
That He spoke to you?

Or choose to forget
And go on your way,
Then stand before Him
on your judgment day.

Where the book He wrote
will by Him be read,
And you will be judged
by what He has said.

www.ingramcontent.com/pod-product-compliance
Lightning Source LLC
Chambersburg PA
CBHW021211020426
42331CB00003B/309